DONALD
TRUMP

45th US President

BY A. R. CARSER

CONTENT CONSULTANT
DR. RACHEL BLUM
ASSISTANT PROFESSOR OF POLITICAL SCIENCE
MIAMI UNIVERSITY, OXFORD, OHIO

Essential Library

An Imprint of Abdo Publishing | abdopublishing.com

abdopublishing.com

Published by Abdo Publishing, a division of ABDO, PO Box 398166, Minneapolis, Minnesota 55439. Copyright © 2017 by Abdo Consulting Group, Inc. International copyrights reserved in all countries. No part of this book may be reproduced in any form without written permission from the publisher. Essential Library™ is a trademark and logo of Abdo Publishing.

Printed in the United States of America, North Mankato, Minnesota
112016
092016

Cover Photo: Carrie Nelson/Dreamstime
Interior Photos: Alex Wong/Getty Images News/Getty Images, 4; Lev Radin/
Shutterstock Images, 8; IBL/Rex Features/AP Images, 10; Bill Clark/CQ Roll Call/AP
Images, 13; Seth Poppel/Yearbook Library, 14, 19; Drew Angerer/Getty Images News/
Getty Images, 17; Dennis Caruso/New York Daily News Archive/Getty, 24; AP Images,
29, 53; Bettmann/Getty Images, 33; Michael Brennan/Hulton Archive/Getty Images,
35; Leif Skoogfors/Corbis Historical/Getty Images, 36; Time & Life Pictures/The LIFE
Picture Collection/Getty Images, 39; Marty Lederhandler/AP Images, 41, 56; Mario
Suriani/AP Images, 43; Wilbur Funches/AP Images, 46; Jon McNally/Hulton Archive/
Getty Images, 50; Hans Deryk/AP Images, 55; NBC/Photofest, 59; Scott Gries/Getty
Images Entertainment/Getty Images, 62; Christopher Gregory/Getty Images News/
Getty Images, 66; iStockphoto, 69; Riccardo Savi/Sipa USA/AP Images, 71; George
Sheldon/Shutterstock Images, 75; Evan Vucci/AP Images, 76, 86; Dennis Van Tine/Sipa
USA/AP Images, 79; John Locher/AP Images, 82, 95; David Goldman/AP Images, 88

Editor: Kate Conley
Series Designer: Becky Daum

Publisher's Cataloging-in-Publication Data

Names: Carser, A. R., author.
Title: Donald Trump: 45th US President / by A. R. Carser.
Description: Minneapolis, MN : Abdo Publishing, [2017] | Series: Essential lives |
    Includes bibliographical references and index.
Identifiers: LCCN 2016942635 | ISBN 9781680783667 (lib. bdg.) |
    ISBN 9781680795189 (ebook)
Subjects: LCSH: Trump, Donald, 1946- --Juvenile literature. | Presidential
    candidates--United States-- Biography--Juvenile literature. | Political
    campaigns--United States--Biography--Juvenile literature. | Presidents--
    United States--Biography--Election, 2016--Juvenile literature.
Classification: DDC 973.932/092 [B]--dc23
LC record available at http://lccn.loc.gov/2016942635

CONTENTS

CHAPTER
ONE

CONVENTION IN CLEVELAND

T he lights dimmed, and "We Are the Champions" by Queen blasted from the speakers at the Quicken Loans Arena in Cleveland, Ohio. A few seconds later, Donald J. Trump strode out, silhouetted by the backlit stage filled with smoke from a fog machine. Clapping, he approached the podium, which rose out of the stage in front of him. "We're gonna win, we're gonna win so big!" Trump exclaimed to the cheering crowd at the Republican National Convention (RNC) on July 18, 2016.[1]

The scene was undeniably dramatic for a political convention, but not surprising given the party's presumptive nominee for president. Trump had spent his entire career as a businessman, creating an image that radiated success, confidence, and drama. Unafraid to boast about his success and his aggressive, competitive business style, Trump capitalized on this brand in his

Never one to shy away from drama, Trump made a memorable entrance at the RNC.

run for the Republican nomination. His personality—and name—were unofficial cornerstones of the RNC.

FROM CEO TO PRESIDENT

Donald Trump often spoke of his business experience during the campaign. He is not the first business leader to run for the office of president. Seven former presidents ran businesses before holding the nation's highest office. Presidents George W. Bush and his father, George H. W. Bush, were both in the oil business. Harry S. Truman owned a men's clothing company. Warren Harding operated a newspaper. Herbert Hoover ran a mining company, and Calvin Coolidge was vice president of a bank in western Massachusetts.

The Road to Cleveland

It had been a long road to the RNC. Trump had begun making stops across the country more than a year before to gauge early support. He formally announced his candidacy on June 16, 2015, while descending the escalator in the lobby of Trump Tower in New York City. In his remarks, he unveiled his campaign slogan, Make America Great Again. He pronounced himself the outsider candidate. He had spent his life making billions of dollars, not serving as a career politician in Washington, DC. This, he said, made him uniquely qualified to make the big changes Americans were increasingly demanding.

Over the past 20 years, American politics had become increasingly polarized. Fewer Americans identified as moderates. Instead, they were identifying with one of the two extremes: conservative or liberal. People in each group felt they had little common ground with those in the other. At the same time, nearly all Americans had become increasingly frustrated with the government. In 2015, only 19 percent of Americans said they trusted the government most or all of the time.[2]

Given this context, it was not surprising that candidates who claimed to be antiestablishment became contenders in the presidential race. Trump became the outsider figure in the Republican race. Bernie Sanders ran against Hillary Clinton as the outsider candidate for the Democrats. Trump and Sanders both appealed to a public that wanted to see a major change in US leaders.

Throughout the primary season, Trump addressed the fears and frustrations of many conservative voters. He promised to increase US jobs. To prevent terrorism, Trump called for a ban on Muslims entering the United States. He also promised to build a wall between the United States and Mexico to stop illegal immigration. Trump planned to cut taxes and leave Social Security benefits as they are.

Trump announced Indiana governor Mike Pence as his running mate two days before the RNC.

The media and establishment Republicans and Democrats alike criticized Trump's plans. They called them contradictory, unconstitutional, and racist. Trump supporters disagreed. Businesswoman Essie Dube summed up the feelings of many Trump supporters when she said, "Donald Trump may be a little rough around the edges . . . but he says it like it is. He says things that other Americans are afraid to say but they feel in their heart."[3]

Nominating Trump

Trump's rallying cries became the major themes at the RNC. The four-day event took place between July 18 and 21, 2016. On the first night, the theme was national security and foreign policy. Soldiers, politicians, actors, and everyday citizens spoke. They shared their experiences of job loss, terrorism, and war. The most noteworthy speech of the night was given by Trump's wife, Melania. She praised her husband's commitment to the United States and his desire to improve the country.

The next morning, the big news story was not about the theme of the RNC's opening night. Instead, it centered on the content of Melania's speech. A paragraph had been plagiarized from a speech First Lady Michelle Obama gave in 2008. The story dominated the news for two days. Trump took to Twitter to address the controversy: "Good news is Melania's speech got more publicity than any in the history of politics especially if you believe that all press is good press!"[4]

The second day of the convention had its share of controversy, too. On that day, delegates planned to vote in the roll call. The vote would formally name Trump as the 2016 presidential nominee. It did not go smoothly.

Melania's speech at the RNC brought attention to Trump's campaign, though not for reasons they expected.

A group of Republicans threatened to get enough delegates to vote to change the party's nominating rules. Doing so would have allowed delegates who had voted for Trump in the primaries to vote for another candidate in the roll call. This is called a contested convention and is rare in modern politics.

These efforts failed, however. Delegates from each state announced their vote totals to the packed arena. Trump's son Donald Trump Jr. was a delegate for the family's home state of New York. He announced New York's votes, which put Trump "over the top" and made him the official Republican nominee for president.

The third night of the convention also made waves when Ted Cruz took the stage. Cruz had been the runner-up to Trump in the primaries. Over the course of his speech, it became clear Cruz would not endorse Trump. Instead, Cruz asked people who were unhappy with Trump as the nominee to "vote your conscience" in November.[5] In effect, he was asking citizens not to vote for Trump. The crowd, which had rallied behind Trump, nearly booed Cruz off the stage.

WHO CAN BE A DELEGATE?

Nearly 2,500 people served as delegates to the Republican National Convention in 2016.[6] They represented all 50 states, Washington, DC, and US territories, such as Guam and Puerto Rico. Each state can choose how its delegates are selected. Some are officials in their state's Republican Party. Other delegates are elected during their state's primary or caucuses. In some states, state party committee members select delegates. In other states, delegates are selected at statewide party meetings.

No matter how they are selected, delegates all meet at the national convention. There, they nominate the Republican Party's presidential candidate. The convention chair leads the vote for the nomination, called a roll call. Each state and territory has the chance to take the floor and announce its votes. Often, delegates also share interesting facts about their home states and territories during this time.

Trump Accepts

On the final night of the RNC, Trump accepted his party's nomination and spoke to the American people. Trump reinforced the themes of his campaign. He promised to lead the United States from crisis to "safety, prosperity, and peace."[7] He said that once he took office, law and order would be restored, US borders would be secured, and America would be great again.

In his acceptance speech, Trump stressed the fact that he was a businessman, not a politician. He admitted that as a businessman, he had learned how what he perceived as the corrupt US government operated. "Nobody knows the system better than me, which is why I alone can fix it," said Trump.[8] Would the American people agree?

"I'M THE LAW AND ORDER CANDIDATE"

Donald Trump made many bold statements in his acceptance speech. Many were in support of maintaining order in towns, cities, and states across the country. Trump pledged that he would work to restore safety and peace to America, which he perceived as a country in crisis. "When I take the oath of office next year, I will restore law and order to our country. . . . In this race to the White House, I am the Law and Order candidate."[9]

At the RNC, Trump spoke about how he could improve the country,
which he believed was headed in the wrong direction.

CHAPTER
TWO

GROWING UP TRUMP

Donald John Trump was born on June 14, 1946, to Mary Anne and Fred Trump. He had two older sisters, Maryanne and Elizabeth. He also had an older brother, Fred Jr., and a younger brother, Robert.

The Trump family lived in the upper-middle-class neighborhood of Jamaica Estates in Queens, New York. When Donald was born, the Trumps lived on Wareham Street in a modest home. But Fred was hard at work on a much larger home on the double lot behind their house. Eventually, it would have 23 rooms and nine bathrooms.[1] The building project was not a new endeavor for Fred. He had been constructing affordable, middle-class apartment complexes and homes in Queens and Brooklyn since the late 1920s.

Trump, *center*, played many sports while in high school.

Fred Trump

Fred was a shrewd businessman and hands-on builder. He was the son of German immigrants who were successful entrepreneurs. His father had started a small real estate business when he moved to Queens in 1908.

When Fred's father died in 1918, Fred aimed to take over the family business. He took construction classes at the local YMCA while finishing high school. After graduating in 1923, he took over the business.

Fred spent the next few years obtaining private loans to fund modest family homes. When the Great Depression reduced demand for homes, Fred opened a grocery store in Queens. He got back into the real estate business in the 1930s, but this time, he did not do it alone. Instead, he built relationships with local

BE A KILLER

Fred Trump was known by his family, friends, and colleagues to be driven, tough, and demanding. He took his business seriously, and he always dressed in a suit and cuff links, even on weekends. Fred was aggressive, arrogant, and pushy in negotiations on the job site and at home. He also took his family's success seriously. Fred pushed Donald to be a "killer," leading by example in his dealings with local politicians and pushing for real estate tax breaks. Donald took these skills with him when he expanded the Trump real estate business into Manhattan.

Trump's childhood home on Wareham Street in Queens, New York

politicians and bankers. They helped him get the best terms for his construction projects. This included taking advantage of new government programs that promoted home ownership, designed to bolster the country's struggling economy.

Young Donald

By the time Donald was born in 1946, Fred was a prominent builder in Queens and Brooklyn. He was also a tireless, driven businessman. During Donald's childhood, Fred worked long hours. He spent 12 to 14 hours every workday visiting building sites and networking with politicians and government officials. Frequently, Donald and his siblings accompanied Fred on weekend trips to job sites, picking up stray nails as their father saved money by performing maintenance himself.

Fred was a taskmaster at home, too. Donald and his siblings had strict curfews and were not allowed to eat between meals. Fred encouraged his children to be mindful of costs at home, just as he did at his job sites. Donald and his siblings had summer jobs, collected bottles to cash in on the deposit, and were encouraged to clean their plates at meals. He also encouraged his children to learn how positive thinking can create success, an idea outlined in the popular book *The Power of Positive Thinking* by minister and author Norman Vincent Peale.

When Donald was five, Fred and Mary Anne enrolled him in a local private school, Kew-Forest School. He was a sociable, outgoing child who got into mischief. At Kew-Forest, he met his childhood best friend, Peter Brant. The two of them soon earned reputations as pranksters, ignoring their studies to shoot spitballs and throw stink bombs. A classmate remembers Donald got in trouble so often that detentions at Kew-Forest

The strict, competitive atmosphere at the New York Military Academy helped shape Trump's character.

became known as DTs, or "Donny Trumps." By the time Donald was 13, the school—and Fred—were fed up with Donald paying more attention to pranks than schoolwork. For eighth grade, Donald would attend the New York Military Academy (NYMA), 55 miles (89 km) from his home.[2]

Thriving with Structure and Competition

The NYMA had a reputation for turning unruly young men into disciplined, successful students. In his five years at the school, that is exactly what happened to Donald. He thrived in the structured environment, where he and his classmates lived in barracks and were awakened by a bugle each morning. In class, in the barracks, and on the sports field, competitiveness and aggression were highly valued at the NYMA. Donald excelled at athletics. As an older student, he was ruthless when it was his job to inspect the barracks.

Summer vacation from the NYMA was not idle time for Donald. Summers were devoted to learning the basics of the family real estate business. He eagerly helped his father on job sites around Queens and Brooklyn. He worked at one of his father's apartment complexes. He was responsible for making sure the building and its units were well maintained. He also drove his dad to and from his daily meetings.

Donald often accompanied his father to Cincinnati, Ohio, where Fred had purchased a rundown apartment complex called Swifton Village. These visits were an education in themselves. Donald observed Fred's drive and tough style with the crews on the job site. Fred allowed Donald to negotiate maintenance contracts with potential vendors and collect rent from reluctant tenants. He emphasized professionalism and the value of hands-on management of job sites.

Off to College

After graduating from the NYMA, Donald enrolled at Fordham University in the Bronx. Donald's studies at Fordham were not going as well as his work with Fred. He had a difficult time fitting in at the school. Donald did not smoke or drink, as did many of his peers, and he had significantly more money than most students at Fordham. In 1966, he transferred to the Wharton School of Business at the University of Pennsylvania.

COLLECTING RENT

During his time at Swifton, Trump collected rent from tenants. The area was rough, and tenants were often reluctant to pay. "One of the first tricks I learned was that you never stand in front of someone's door when you knock," recalled Trump. "Instead you stand by the wall and reach over to knock."[3] One of the men training Trump explained why he should do it this way. "If you stand to the side, the only thing exposed to danger is your hand. . . . In this business, if you knock on the wrong apartment at the wrong time, you're liable to get shot."[4]

The Wharton School had a small but strong real estate department—one of only a few such departments in the nation at the time. Donald competed fiercely with his classmates, most of whom were from real estate families similar to the Trumps. Donald graduated from the Wharton School on May 20, 1968. He walked off the graduation stage and onto the stage of commercial real estate.

THE VIETNAM WAR DRAFT

In June 1964, Donald turned 18 years old. Like all other 18-year-old American men, the law required him to register with the Selective Services System. This government agency keeps track of men eligible for military service. When Donald registered, the United States was fighting in the Vietnam War (1954–1975). A draft looked likely.

Donald received four deferments while in college, one for each year he was a student. It meant he would not have to serve in the military. When Donald graduated in 1968, his deferments ended. The government was poised to call a draft. The fall after graduation, Donald received a medical deferment for bone spurs in his heel. It kept him out of the draft.

The circumstances around Donald's medical deferment are unclear. Critics argue he got a fake diagnosis to avoid being drafted and did not do his patriotic duty. "I think I've made a lot of sacrifices," he said in response to the accusations. "I work very, very hard. I've created thousands and thousands of jobs, tens of thousands of jobs, built great structures. I've had tremendous success. I think I've done a lot."[5]

Starting Out at Swifton

Donald's first job after college was managing his father's Swifton Village apartment complex. When Fred purchased the rundown 1,200-unit apartment complex in 1964, only 66 percent of the apartments were rented.[6] Fred's company had renovated the property, and two years later the apartment complex was full. Now, it was his son's turn to manage the property.

Donald moved to Cincinnati to manage Swifton Village. He spent his first summer after college supervising projects on the property. Employees remember Donald rolling up his sleeves and helping with landscaping and other projects. In his 1987 book, *The Art of the Deal*, he describes the turnaround of Swifton Village as his first big deal. But Donald had his sights set on something much bigger. He dreamed of developing real estate in Manhattan.

CHAPTER
THREE

BUILDING NEW YORK

After a summer focusing on Swifton Village, Trump shifted his attention to helping his father with the New York properties. His main role was collecting rent from tenants of Trump Management Corporation properties. The company owned and managed thousands of apartments in Staten Island, Queens, and Brooklyn. Trump describes the experience of going door-to-door to collect rent as unpleasant and, at times, violent.

In 1973, Trump became the president of Trump Management Corporation. The company owned more than 14,000 apartments in Queens, Brooklyn, and Staten Island, New York.[1]

The Trump Philosophy

Though he had an Ivy League business degree, Trump's business philosophy came from his father.

Trump learned many of the skills he needed in real estate from his father, Fred.

The hard-driving builder worked tirelessly to develop his real estate business. His specialty was renovating rundown properties. He made them appeal to working-class families who hoped to move up to the middle class. Always a frugal man, he improved a property's quality without adding frivolous extras. Fred demanded work be done precisely and cost-effectively.

Fred looked for ways to bring the cost of properties down. Early on, he realized the best way to reduce costs was to negotiate tax breaks for his projects. It was not an easy task. To do it, he spent time getting to know New York's most powerful politicians. He funded campaigns for governor and Congress. He sat on powerful boards, such as the one for the Brooklyn Borough Gas Company. All of this earned Fred influence with local politicians. In turn, they made it easier for him to make profitable

FRUGAL FRED

When Fred Trump died in 1999, Donald Trump shared a story about his father that illustrated Fred's frugality and ingenuity. The thousands of apartments Trump Management maintained required the company to buy cleaning products in bulk. But the cost of these products added up. Trump remembers finding his father in his office, his desk covered in bottles of floor cleaner. Fred sent the bottles to a lab to discover their chemical formulas and then used the results to create his own. Instead of paying two dollars a bottle, he paid fifty cents.[2]

deals on properties. When his son entered the family business, Donald inherited these connections.

A Federal Lawsuit

These connections made the work easier, but it was not always smooth going. On the morning of October 15, 1973, Trump received a distressing phone call. The US Department of Justice was on the line warning him it was filing a lawsuit against Trump Management Corporation for violating the Fair Housing Act of 1968.

The Fair Housing Act made it illegal for landlords to discriminate on the basis of race, color, religion, gender, or national origin. The lawsuit alleged Trump Management refused to rent apartments to African Americans. It also charged that the company had offered potential tenants different lease terms depending on the color of their skin.

In his first time quoted in the *New York Times* newspaper, Trump declared the charges "absolutely ridiculous."[3] He hired his friend and attorney Roy Cohn to represent Trump Management. Cohn sued the US government over irresponsible and baseless charges that singled out Trump Management because it was a large, successful company.

The government and Trump Management resolved the lawsuit in a 1975 agreement. In it, Trump Management agreed to supply the New York Urban League, a group representing disadvantaged New Yorkers, with a list of vacant apartments every week for two years. The agreement also made it clear that Trump Management was not guilty of the charges brought against it.

Making a Mark on Manhattan

By the time the lawsuit was resolved, Trump had begun making his mark on Manhattan. At the time, Manhattan's economy was struggling. Many properties were in distress, including high-profile ones such as the Chrysler Building and Grand Central Terminal. Fred had no interest in taking a gamble on these buildings. But his son saw opportunity. Trump persuaded Fred to financially support his foray into Manhattan real estate.

In 1976, Trumps purchased his first Manhattan property, the bankrupt Commodore Hotel. In making the deal, Trump took a move out of his father's playbook, using tax laws to his advantage. He pressed city officials to provide huge tax breaks for the project. In exchange, his new hotel would improve a rundown

Trump, *left*, worked with influential politicians such as New York City mayor Ed Koch, *center*, New York governor Hugh Carey, *pointing*, and executive Robert T. Dormer, *right*, to complete the Commodore Hotel project.

part of the city. Trump's Commodore Hotel project became Manhattan's first commercial property to receive a 40-year tax abatement from the government.[4]

Work began on the project in 1978. Workers gutted the Commodore and renovated it into a 1,400-room hotel that appealed to wealthy guests. It opened two years later as the Grand Hyatt Hotel. For the work, Manhattan's Community Board Five gave Trump an award for the "tasteful and creative recycling of a distinguished hotel."[5] The project revitalized the neighborhood. It also gave Trump a taste of the opportunity that awaited him in the Manhattan housing market.

A Young Family

The 1970s were not all work for Trump. Over the decade, he had cultivated a reputation as a young, hot-shot builder. He belonged to clubs that catered to the wealthy and drove a Cadillac with the license plate "DJT"—his initials.

In 1976, Trump met Ivana Winklmayr. Born in Czechoslovakia, Winklmayr was a skier and fashion model. She moved to New York in 1976 to continue her modeling career. She and Trump married on April 9, 1977, after dating for nine months. On December 31, the couple welcomed its first child, Donald John Trump Jr.

Project T

Trump's next big endeavor was the Bonwit Teller building. It had housed the Bonwit Teller & Co. department store between 1930 and 1979. The building was a well-known example of art deco design, with large limestone carvings worked into the facade of the building. This is not what attracted Trump, though. He was interested in the building's prime location, surrounded by high-end shops just three blocks from Central Park.

Trump began secret negotiations to acquire the building in 1979, calling the deal Project T. He took over the building's lease and obtained the right to rename it. In negotiations, Trump argued for an exception to the city's zoning code. He wanted to build a tower that would give tenants a two-sided view: one of Central Park and another of southern Manhattan. Such a building did not fit the strict rules that required new structures to fit into the neighborhood. To win the exception, Trump offered a second design that violated the zoning rules to an outrageous degree. The planning commission accepted Trump's first plan and waived the zoning rule.

In 1980, demolition began on Project T, which would later become known as Trump Tower. Not all went smoothly, though. Trump had hired the contractor Kaszycki & Sons to perform the demolition. The contractor had come in with the lowest bid for the work. It soon became obvious why the bid was so low. Kaszycki & Sons hired undocumented Polish immigrants, paying

FACADE FIASCO

Since its construction in 1929, the Bonwit Tower had become a prominent building due to its striking facade. Two large limestone panels were examples of art deco design and featured two dancing women who stood 15 feet (4.6 m) tall.[6] When the building went up for sale, art and architecture historians hoped to preserve the artwork.

When Trump started work on Trump Tower, he promised to donate the building's historic limestone facade to the Metropolitan Museum of Art.

But after a few months, the artful facade had been jackhammered away. Removing the panels was much more expensive than Trump had anticipated. It would also have led to costly delays, which would have hampered his ability to secure a highly valuable tax abatement on the project. Without the abatement, the project would have cost Trump $25 million more.[7] Art lovers and historians were outraged by Trump's decision.

Before completing a building, developers work with models of their designs, such as this one of Trump Tower.

them less than half what union workers would get. The Polish workers toiled 12 to 18 hours a day, seven days a week, without hard hats.[8] In 1983, the workers sued both Kaszycki & Sons and Trump. The FBI investigated to see if the immigrant workers had been taken advantage of. The case was finally settled out of court in 1999.

Work continued on Trump Tower. In July 1982, 700 people, including the governor and mayor of New York City, toasted its near completion. To celebrate, they rode a construction elevator to the top of the building for a brunch.

Soon, Trump Tower started selling apartments to wealthy buyers. Trump spared no expense, bathing the building in luxury. High-end finishes adorned the apartments, but the showstopper was Trump Tower's public lobby. Rose-colored marble covered the floor and walls, and mirrors made the space seem large. A waterfall splashed down one wall of the lobby, inviting shoppers into the building's high-end boutiques. Perched atop all this luxury was Trump's personal 53-room penthouse.[9]

The twenty-sixth floor of Trump Tower houses Trump's corporate offices.

CHAPTER
FOUR

GAMBLING ON THE FUTURE

Trump had made an impression on the real estate world in New York. Meanwhile, he had already begun his next project in Atlantic City, New Jersey. The city had just legalized gambling in 1978, and Trump saw an opportunity to make money there.

Trump bid on the largest lot on the strip in Atlantic City. The lot was actually three separate properties and involved 30 property owners.[1] Trump was new to the casino business, but he knew if he followed the strict local rules and regulations, he stood to make a great deal of money as a casino owner. He began construction on a casino, Trump Plaza, in 1982.

Harrah's, an established casino and resort company, was looking to partner with a builder to develop its first Atlantic City property. In 1984, the partners opened a casino called Harrah's at Trump Plaza. The next year, the partnership between Trump and Harrah's collapsed.

In the 1980s, Trump believed casinos were a solid investment, and he put much of his wealth into developing them.

Meanwhile, Trump had been in secret negotiations with Hilton Hotel Corporation. It was a competitor of Harrah's. Trump partnered with Hilton to buy another casino, which he renamed Trump Castle. This outraged Harrah's. After some public mudslinging, Trump bought out Harrah's stake in Trump Plaza.

Trump continued to invest in casinos, and in 1987 he bought a majority share in Resorts International Inc. The deal included high-risk bonds and two casinos. One casino was in the Bahamas. The other, the Taj Mahal, was still under construction in Atlantic City. Two years later, Trump sold his shares in Resorts International but kept the casinos. He had run out of money, and selling Resorts International helped him avoid bankruptcy.

IVANA TRUMP, CEO

In 1985, Trump made Ivana the CEO of Trump Castle in Atlantic City. The move ensured operations remained in the family. At the time, she had no experience running a casino. But the competitive and determined Ivana did not let lack of experience deter her. Taking a cue from her husband, Ivana actively managed Trump Castle, reviewing every detail personally and even signing the checks herself. A natural hostess, Ivana organized successful parties for the casino's high rollers. Under her leadership, Trump Castle thrived. Its revenues soon outpaced those of Trump's other Atlantic City casino, Trump Plaza.

Ivana and Trump both worked while their children, including Ivanka, *left*, and Donald Jr., *right*, were growing up.

Three Costly Projects

Trump's next project brought him back to Manhattan. He was interested in a 77-acre (31 ha) property known as the Yards, which ran along the Hudson River.[2] Trump had purchased the property briefly in the 1970s but was forced to sell when he did not have the funds to build on it. Now, in 1982, Trump had bought back the property and proposed a giant new project: Television City.

The plans called for several luxury skyscrapers, including a tower that would have become the tallest in the world. But the largest part of the development would be space for television studios, a shopping mall, and a giant parking lot. Television City would be the largest project undertaken in New York City since Rockefeller Center in the 1930s. Opposition from neighborhood groups and city planners put Television City on hold.

In the meantime, Trump had expanded his real estate holdings south to Palm Beach, Florida. In 1985, he purchased the $10 million mansion and beach property called Mar-a-Lago.[3] The property formerly belonged to a prominent Palm Beach family but had fallen into disrepair. Trump renovated the property, turning it into a luxury resort with a high price tag for membership. He included a private area for the use of his family.

Three years later, Trump set his sights on another property: the Plaza Hotel in Manhattan, across from Central Park and near

MAR-A-LAGO

In 1995, Mar-a-Lago, Trump's personal estate in Palm Beach, Florida, opened its doors as a private club for the wealthy. Welcomed by a larger-than-life painting of Trump, members paid $25,000 to join the exclusive club, a cost that has since increased.[4] Members enjoy luxurious accommodations, fine dining, a spa, a golf course, and other recreational activities.

The land for Television City was the largest undeveloped lot in Manhattan. Trump's plan included a 150-story tower. Complaints from neighbors stopped the plan in 1987.

Trump Tower. Trump paid $407.5 million for the Plaza Hotel, the highest price ever for a single hotel.[5] He also put a $125 million guarantee on the loan he took out to pay for the plaza.[6] It was a move unheard of in the real estate industry. It meant Trump would personally be responsible for $125 million if the project failed.[7]

Family Matters

The early 1980s were a time of major change for the Trump family. In September 1981, Fred Trump Jr. died at age 42 after a long battle with alcoholism. His death profoundly upset Trump, who had avoided consuming alcohol after seeing its destructive effects on his older brother.

A month after Fred Jr.'s death, Ivana and Donald welcomed another Trump heir into the family. Ivanka Trump was born on October 30, 1981. She was the couple's second child. Eric Trump was born three years later on January 6, 1984.

Donald Jr., Ivanka, and Eric had a sheltered upbringing typical of a billionaire family. With Donald and Ivana away making real estate deals and managing job sites, the children spent much of their time with nannies. The three children were close growing up and remain so as adults.

The Art of the Deal

By 1987, Trump had made multimillion-dollar deals on real estate in New York, New Jersey, and Florida. He had his own air shuttle, called Trump Airlines, and

Trump expanded his brand in many ways, including creating a board game called Trump: The Game in 1989. To play, opponents bid against each other to make real estate deals.

lived his business and personal lives in the public eye. The press loved reporting stories of Trump's outrageous lifestyle and business deals. There was no better time to release a book cataloging his success.

Trump hired *New York Magazine* writer Tony Schwartz to ghostwrite his first book, *The Art of the Deal.*

The book describes the details of Trump's most successful business deals. It showcases Trump's public persona, which was brazen, optimistic, and showy. At times, he also had a knack for stretching the truth to make himself look good.

Trump announced the publication of the book on December 12, 1987, with a celebrity-laden party at Trump Tower. *The Art of the Deal* immediately became a best seller. It sold more than 1 million copies and remained on the *New York Times* bestseller

ALL IN THE FAMILY

Trump learned about the real estate business from his father, and he taught his own children in the same way. His three oldest children—Donald Jr., Ivanka, and Eric—are all senior executives in Trump's real estate business. As Trump's bid for president became more serious, his children took on high-profile roles in the campaign. "In business and politics, we obviously influence our father's thought process, but he always makes up his own mind," said Donald Jr. "Ivanka, Eric and I have the ability to be very candid with our father."[8]

list for 48 weeks.[9] It also exposed Trump and his ideas to the whole country.

Stepping into Politics

Riding high on his success, Trump entered the world of politics. He had worked with the politicians of New York and Atlantic City for more than a decade. In 1987, he considered running in the 1988 presidential election.

To test his support, he took out full-page ads in the *New York Times*, the *Boston Globe*, and the *Washington Post*. In them, Trump offered to negotiate arms deals with the Soviet Union on behalf of President Ronald Reagan. "There's nothing wrong with America's Foreign Defense Policy that a little backbone can't cure," the ad stated.[10]

The ad triggered speculation that Trump was thinking of running for president. Research showed he could be a serious contender in the Republican primary. Trump never formally announced his candidacy, and a speech in New Hampshire was as far as his presidential bid went. But it would not be the last time Trump would stand in the political spotlight.

CHAPTER
FIVE

BUILDING
THE BRAND

An integral part of Trump's success in the 1980s had been his ability to sell himself as a successful real estate developer. As his success grew, he bought personal property, such as a yacht, mansions, limos, and personal jets. His own luxury lifestyle had become an integral aspect of Trump the businessman. He had a reputation as one of New York's top real estate developers and richest residents.

The success came at a cost, though. Trump had spent the 1980s acquiring properties to develop. But Trump did not pay for these properties with his own money. He had borrowed hundreds of millions of dollars to fund Trump Tower, Atlantic City, Mar-a-Lago, and the Plaza Hotel. In the 1990s, Trump struggled to repay the money he owed. The next ten years would be tumultuous ones for the New York billionaire.

Trump's helicopter, yacht, mansions, and other luxurious assets helped build his reputation of success.

PAYING FOR PROPERTIES

Most real estate developers do not have millions of dollars in cash stored in bank accounts they use to purchase properties. Instead, they rely on loans from big banks to fund their projects. The banks put up their own money to pay for the construction, which the developers pay back over time once their buildings are open for business. Often, cities offer real estate companies incentives for developing properties. Trump received special tax abatements for many of his Manhattan properties, reducing the amount of tax he owed. On high-value properties, abatements can save developers tens of millions of dollars.

Bankruptcy Hits

Trump's luxurious Taj Mahal casino finally opened in Atlantic City in 1990. It had financial problems from the start. Trump struggled to keep up with the interest payments on the loans that paid for the work on the Taj Mahal.

In December 1990, Trump's father bought 700 poker chips worth $3.5 million at the Taj Mahal. The Casino Control Commission fined the Taj Mahal $65,000 for allowing the purchase.[1] The commission suggested Fred never intended to play the chips. Instead, it alleged the $3.5 million purchase put much-needed cash into the casino's bank account.[2] Fred had, in effect, given the casino an interest-free loan. It violated the casino laws in Atlantic City.

In 1991, Trump was fined again. This time it was for giving gifts to a client who played millions of dollars at Trump's casinos. The client was Robert Libutti, an alleged Mafia member. Trump pulled out all the stops for Libutti. He bought Libutti nine luxury cars, including Ferraris, Rolls Royces, and Bentleys. This violated another casino law, and Trump had to pay $450,000 in fines.[3]

The casino fines added to losses from his airline, hotels, and other investments. Combined with large interest payments, these debts drained Trump's bank accounts. He filed for bankruptcy in 1991. In bankruptcy negotiations, Trump gave up half of his ownership in the Taj Mahal and sold his yacht and Trump Airlines. The bankruptcy deal also forced Trump to follow a personal spending limit, but the Taj Mahal was able to keep its doors open.

The next year, Trump's other casino in Atlantic City, Trump Plaza, put Trump in further debt. It had lost $550 million, and to avoid shutting its doors, Trump once again filed for bankruptcy.[4] In the deal, Trump kept his CEO title but lost his stake in the casino and his salary. After the two bankruptcies, Trump personally owed lenders approximately $900 million.[5]

Throughout 1980s and 1990s, Trump spent many hours leading board meetings for the companies he owned.

Comeback

Trump later reflected on this difficult time in his book *The Art of the Comeback*. According to Trump, he had turned over important decisions to employees. He had pulled back from the day-to-day details of running his business and was no longer using his instincts. As he realized this, he worked to rebuild his business.

In 1993, Trump reassured the press that he had had one of his most successful years ever. Newspapers reported Trump was making a comeback. In 1995, he purchased 40 Wall Street for $1 million.[6] It was a rundown office building in the heart of New York's financial district. After investing $35 million in renovations, the historic building would be worth $500 million 20 years later.[7]

But Trump's major success of the 1990s was the renovation at the Penn Central rail yards, where he had once envisioned Television City. To fund the project, Trump made a deal with investors from Hong Kong. The Hong Kong group purchased the property, but Trump would oversee the property's development and lend his name to the project. In 1997, ground broke on the first of seven apartment towers at Trump Place.

"I got a little cocky and, probably, a little bit lazy. I wasn't working as hard, and I wasn't focusing on the basics. . . . I began to socialize more, probably too much. Frankly, I was bored. I really felt I could do no wrong. Sort of like a baseball player who keeps hitting home runs . . . My blip—as I call my difficult time—was much different from that of my friends. It was more a sabbatical of sorts. If I'd had my eye on the ball, I'm sure I would have seen more of the problems on the economic horizon."[8]

—Donald Trump,
The Art of the Comeback

SELLING THE GRAND HYATT

Throughout the boom in the 1980s and the bust of the early 1990s, Trump had kept his 50 percent share of the property that launched his career: the Grand Hyatt. But his partnership with the Hyatt Corporation was always rocky, especially during Trump's 1991 and 1992 bankruptcies. The deteriorating relationship culminated in lawsuits in 1993. In 1996, Trump sold his interest in the Grand Hyatt to the Hyatt Corporation for $140 million. Though he gave up ownership of his first major project, he had turned a profit on his $100 million investment.[9]

Trouble at Home

Just as the 1990s had been a rocky period for his business, Trump's personal life also faced many ups and downs. Trump began a secret affair with model and actress Marla Maples. By Christmas 1989, the secret was out. Two weeks later, Ivana filed for divorce. The press extensively covered their high-profile breakup, which included the division of multimillion-dollar properties and millions in assets.

Trump and Maples married in December 1993 at the Plaza Hotel. Two months earlier, they had welcomed a daughter, Tiffany. But the marriage did not last. In 1997, the couple announced they were splitting, formally divorcing in 1999. Marla and Tiffany moved

Trump and Ivana celebrated her US citizenship in May 1988. Ivana had moved from Czechoslovakia to the United States in 1976.

to Los Angeles, California, while Trump remained in New York.

In 1999, Trump suffered another personal loss. His father died on June 25 at age 93 after a battle with Alzheimer's disease. Fred left behind an estate worth between $250 million and $300 million.[10] Speaking at his father's funeral, Trump described the day as the toughest of his life.

With the loss of his father, two divorces, and bankruptcy, the 1990s had been tumultuous years for Trump. But ever the salesman, he would move forward into the new century promoting his success. A host of new business ventures would cement him as a household name across the United States.

Trump and Marla's daughter, Tiffany, was born in West Palm Beach, Florida, on October 13, 1993.

CHAPTER
SIX

BRANCHING OUT

As 1999 came to a close, Trump was considering a run for the presidency. Trump's friend Roger Stone, an experienced political adviser, encouraged him. Stone suggested the mood of the country was shifting, and this could be Trump's moment for victory.

The changes had begun seven years earlier. Independent candidate Ross Perot won 19 percent of the votes in the 1992 presidential election.[1] He was a billionaire with no political experience, yet he earned a respectable number of votes. In 1995, he started the Reform Party. Then in 1998, Reform candidate Jesse Ventura won election as governor of Minnesota. Similar to Perot, Ventura had no political experience.

Stone thought Trump could have success with the Reform Party, too. In October 1999, Trump joined the Reform Party. As time went on, Trump was not confident a Reform Party candidate could win a presidential election. Trump dropped out of the race in February 2000. Though it ended quickly, Trump's

The Reform Party is still a
presence in American politics
today. The party operates
on the idea that only a small
percentage of Americans
are on the far left or the far
right of the political spectrum,
and most are in the middle.
The Reform Party believes
the majority of Americans
in the middle are poorly
represented by Democrats
and Republicans. It is the
group in the middle that
Reform candidates attempt to
win over. The governorship
is the highest office in which
a Reform candidate has
served. Other state and local
offices have been filled by
Reform candidates as well.

presidential bid was the first in
a series of pursuits outside of
real estate.

"You're Fired!"

In 2002, reality television
producer Mark Burnett pitched
an idea to Trump. Burnett
thought Trump's larger-than-life
personality could make a
business reality show a
hit. Trump agreed, and he
negotiated a salary of $100,000
per show and half interest in the
show itself.[2] With his name and
his business being showcased
on every episode, Trump knew
the show would help build the
Trump brand.

Called *The Apprentice*, Burnett's show pitted
contestants against each other for the opportunity
to run one of Trump's businesses. Trump was the
show's boss, deciding who would continue on and who
would be fired. When the show premiered in 2004, it

In the boardroom of *The Apprentice*, Trump, with the help of advisers, decided who would continue to the next episode.

became an instant hit. Millions of viewers tuned in to watch. Charismatic, brazen, and blunt, Trump became a favorite with viewers. He even coined the show's signature catchphrase "You're fired!"

The Apprentice made Trump a household name nationwide. So did the various spin-off products he licensed in the wake of the show's success. Soon, fans could buy Trump suits and ties, fragrances, and even bottled water. Trump was no longer known as just a real estate developer.

Atlantic City and Chicago

While Trump enjoyed his newfound success as a television personality, all was not well with his real estate investments. Trump's Atlantic City casinos had accumulated $1.8 billion in debt.[3] To avoid collapse, Trump filed for bankruptcy.

In the proceedings, Trump was able to reduce the interest rates on his debts. He also secured a $500 million loan to improve the properties so they could become more profitable.[4] In return, Trump had to reduce his personal stake in the company to just 25 percent.[5] This meant he no longer had exclusive control over the company. In 2009, Trump was back in bankruptcy court. To save the company, Trump had to resign as chairman of the board.

Never one to be deterred, Trump continued looking for new projects. In 2005, Trump purchased the Chicago Sun-Times building in Chicago, Illinois, for $73 million.[6] His renovations transformed it into the city's second-tallest building. Renamed the Trump International Hotel and Tower, it contained condominiums, a luxury hotel, shops, and restaurants.

During these years, Trump was dating former Slovenian model Melania Knauss. The two married on January 22, 2005. They had a glamorous, celebrity-filled reception at Trump's Mar-a-Lago property. In 2006, the couple welcomed their first child, Barron.

Trump University

Trump had become a successful real estate developer and television personality and had even stepped onto the political stage. In 2005, he rolled out a new venture, Trump University, entering the field of education for the first time.

Trump University courses were intended to help students make money in the real estate industry using Trump's methods. The seminars were taught

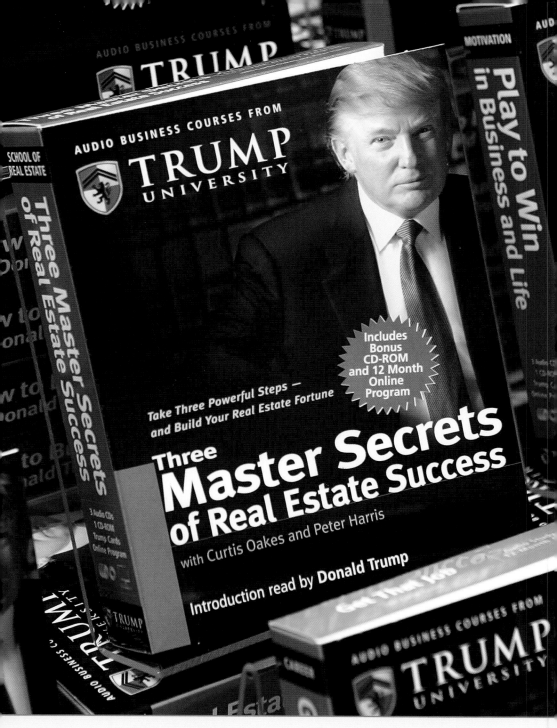

In 2006, Trump University released a series of nine audio courses on how to succeed in business. The series featured advice directly from Trump himself.

by instructors the school claimed Trump had handpicked. The first session was free. Then instructors urged students to purchase a three-day seminar for approximately $1,500 to learn all of Trump's strategies.[7] Next, the instructors offered mentorships to their students for $35,000.[8]

After five years in operation, Trump University was sued by several former students. The students claimed the school was actually an infomercial. Its aim was to persuade students to pay thousands of dollars for generic business strategies that had nothing to do with Trump. In the aftermath of the lawsuit, Trump University was forced to change its name to Trump Entrepreneur Initiative. It closed just one year later.

"Birtherism"

In 2011, Trump once again entered the political arena. Trump kicked off an unofficial bid for president by challenging the truth of Barack Obama's birth certificate. Trump claimed Obama was not born in the United States and was therefore ineligible to be president, according to the US Constitution.

This theory became known as "birtherism." Trump demanded Obama present his birth certificate as proof that he was born in this country. At first, Obama dismissed Trump and the birthers. But Trump continued pressing the president on the issue. He appeared on morning talk shows to discuss his theory and repeat his demand that Obama make his birth certificate public.

The more Trump pushed the birth issue, the higher he rose in the polls. At one point, he had nearly reached the top. In April, after six weeks of demands, Trump finally got his wish. President Obama released a copy of his birth certificate that proved he was born in Honolulu, Hawaii.

THE TROUBLE CONTINUES

The trouble over Trump University continued even after the school closed in 2010. In 2013, New York attorney general Eric Schneiderman filed a lawsuit against Trump. It alleged that the school had misled students in an attempt to make money. In short, the attorney general claimed the school was a fraud.

The suit was still being deliberated in the fall of 2016. While on the campaign trail, Trump attacked the federal judge presiding over the case, Gonzalo Curiel. Curiel was born in Indiana and of Mexican heritage. Trump accused Curiel of bias in the case because he was of Mexican heritage, and Trump had plans to build a wall along the US-Mexico border.

The comment sparked outrage in the media and among voters and dozens of politicians Republican and Democratic alike. At first, Trump defended his statement. But it hurt him in the polls. After the attack, approximately 66 percent of Americans believed Trump was unfit to be president.[9] Trump later distanced himself from the issue.

Over the next month, Trump's polling numbers started to sink. By mid-May, his disapproval rating sank to 64 percent.[10] On May 16, Trump formally announced that he would not run for president. "The decision does not come easily or without regret," he said. "I maintain the strong conviction that if I were to run, I would be able to win the primary and ultimately, the general election," he added.[11] In four years, he would try his hand again.

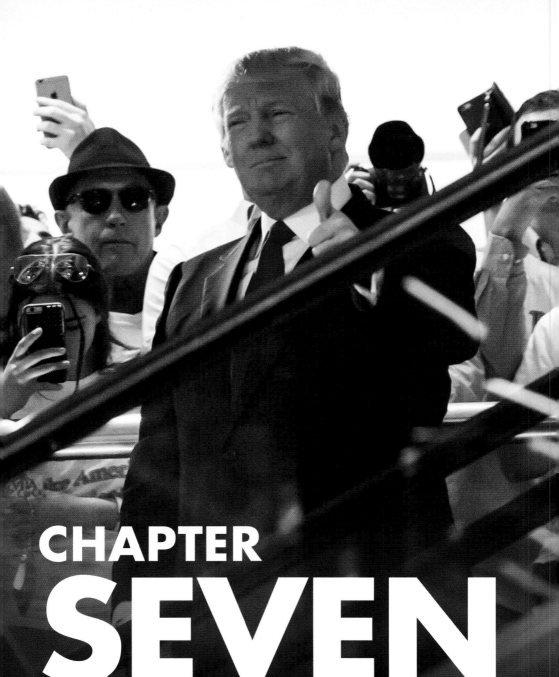

CHAPTER
SEVEN

MAKE AMERICA GREAT AGAIN

On June 16, 2015, Trump descended the escalator at Trump Tower to a waiting crowd in the skyscraper's lobby. He announced that he was officially running for president of the United States. He promised to use his business know-how to improve the country. And, he would fund the campaign with his own money.

"Our country needs a truly great leader, and we need a truly great leader now," Trump told the crowd. "We need a leader that can bring back our jobs, can bring back our manufacturing, can bring back our military, can take care of our vets. . . . We need somebody that can take the brand of the United States and make it great again."[1]

The tone of Trump's speech reflected his aggressive style. He hit hard against President Obama as well as his fellow Republican candidates. Trump spoke forcefully about trade, terrorism, and immigration.

Trump's comments about immigration drew harsh criticism. He suggested some Mexican immigrants entering the United States were violent criminals. He also promised he would build a wall along the US-Mexico border to keep immigrants from crossing unlawfully—and he would make Mexico pay for it.

The Latino community and the press were outraged. Trump's fellow Republican candidates criticized the comments. NBC and Univision cut ties with Trump. Rather than apologize, Trump doubled down on his views. The wall and his stance on immigration would become cornerstones of his candidacy.

Trump's controversial positions drew protesters at his rallies, speeches, and the RNC.

Controversy Continues

On December 2, 2015, the topic of immigration appeared in the news again. That day, Tashfeen Malik and Syed Farook shot and killed 14 people and injured 22 others at a holiday party in San Bernardino, California.[3] Malik was a Muslim immigrant from Pakistan. Farook, her husband, was a US citizen and radical Muslim.

When asked about the attack, Trump had a strong response. He called for a ban on all Muslims entering the United States, whether immigrants or visitors. "Until we are able to determine and understand this problem and the dangerous threat it poses, our country cannot be the victims of horrendous attacks by people that believe only in Jihad, and have no sense of reason or respect for human life," said Trump.[4]

The press, along with Democratic and Republican leaders alike, criticized Trump's position. They said it would be a violation of international law. It was against the principles the nation was founded upon. Many leaders said it was tearing apart the nation, rather than bringing it together. And Trump's idea would be difficult, if not impossible, to enforce.

> "One thing I've learned about the press is that they're always hungry for a good story, and the more sensational the better. . . . The point is that if you are a little different, or a little outrageous, or if you do things that are bold and controversial, the press is going to write about you. I've always done things a little differently, I don't mind controversy, and my deals tend to be somewhat ambitious. . . . The result is that the press has always wanted to write about me."[7]
>
> —Donald Trump,
> The Art of the Deal

Picking Up Speed

In the quest for the Republican nomination, Trump had 17 rivals.[5] It was the largest field of candidates for one party in modern history.[6] Only 12 stayed in the race to the first primary battle, the Iowa caucuses on February 1, 2016.

Presidential candidates, *left to right*, Ben Carson, Marco Rubio, Trump, Ted Cruz, and John Kasich were the front-runners of the Republican Party in early 2016.

It determined the leading contenders for the party's nomination.[8]

Senator Ted Cruz won the Iowa caucuses by more than three percentage points. Trump finished second. Trump said his strong finish was an honor. He also noted that most polls and experts had predicted he would earn few votes in the state.

Trump soon started winning state after state. He won the next four contests in New Hampshire, South Carolina, Nevada, and Alabama. Then came March 1—Super Tuesday, when 11 states held their

Republican contests. Trump won seven of them, many by wide margins.[9]

After Super Tuesday, Trump was on fire. He won 26 of the remaining 38 contests, with rivals Ted Cruz, Marco Rubio, and John Kasich each winning a handful of the rest of the states and territories.[10] Rubio dropped out of the race on March 16 after he lost the primary of his home state, Florida.

By May, Cruz and Kasich realized they could not win enough delegates to get the nomination. Cruz dropped out on May 3, and Kasich did the same the next day. In the end, Trump had earned the pledges of 1,447 delegates during the primary and caucus season.[11] This was 210 more delegates than he needed to secure the nomination at the Republican National Convention in July.[12]

Defying Convention

As a sharp-spoken Washington outsider, Trump soon set the tone for the rhetoric used during the Republican primary contest. Most candidates carefully consider the public remarks they make. Trump, on the other hand, thrived on spontaneity. He was blunt, aggressive, and sometimes offensive. He jumped from thought to thought quickly, often leaving sentences unfinished. Many voters liked this casual style, even if later some of his facts were proven incorrect.

Trump used his trademark rhetoric at the first Republican primary debates on August 6, 2015. Moderator Megyn Kelly asked about negative comments he had made about women. Trump's response centered on how the nation should worry less about being politically correct. He also took a shot at Kelly, saying he had treated her nicely even though she did not always deserve it.

TRUMP AND THE PRESS

Throughout his campaign, Trump had a complicated relationship with the national press. As he did as a businessman, Trump used free coverage from the media to communicate his positions and agenda. His experience as a television host made him an engaging and entertaining subject. By March 15, Trump had received nearly $2 billion in free media coverage in just the first nine months of his campaign. That was more than six times that of Ted Cruz, his closest rival.[13]

Though he enjoyed regular interviews and intense coverage of his rallies, Trump took a hard line against what he saw as media biased against him and his conservative supporters. He insulted and sometimes threatened journalists who challenged him on his positions during press conferences. He banned several news organizations from attending his campaign events. Trump also vowed that as president, he would change the nation's laws to make it easier to sue newspapers for "purposely negative" articles.[14]

The discussion continued after the debate. Trump struck out at Kelly once again in an interview, claiming her challenge was out of line. "She gets out and she starts asking me all sorts of ridiculous questions. You could see there was blood coming out of her eyes, blood coming out of her wherever."[15] The claim, which most agreed was referring to the moderator's menstrual cycle, caused an uproar in the press. The next month, Trump disparaged fellow candidate Carly Fiorina in an interview, exclaiming, "Look at that face! Would anyone vote for that?"[16] The comment again sparked outrage.

Telling It Like It Is

Over the next few months, Trump aimed more verbal attacks against his opponents. He also called out people and ideas he considered threats to the United States. Trump asserted that as president, he would bomb the territory and oil refineries of the terrorist organization ISIS until there was nothing left. He also made up disparaging nicknames for his primary opponents. Some of these attacks were made on the primary debate stage, but many others were made in press interviews, on Trump's preferred social media platform, Twitter, and at his campaign rallies.

Trump's supporters appreciated the way he spoke without fear of being politically correct.

Trump's inflammatory rhetoric did not dampen support for him. Supporters appreciated Trump's willingness to "tell it like it is" on issues, despite his assertions being unpopular in the press. They felt Trump was unafraid to say what they believed to be true on issues such as law enforcement, immigration, and the economy.

By May, Trump was the last one standing and had become the presumptive nominee. In July, Republicans would formally nominate him at the Republican National Convention. He had won the primary contest. Could he win the presidency?

CHAPTER
EIGHT

THE CAMPAIGN TRAIL

B y the time the RNC began, Trump had been the Republican presumptive nominee for more than two months. During that time, some Republican voters and prominent Republican leaders rallied behind his candidacy. Notably, Speaker of the House Paul Ryan endorsed Trump's candidacy in early June.

Other political leaders remained skeptical, including the former Republican presidential nominees Mitt Romney and John McCain. Former Republican presidents George W. Bush and George H. W. Bush did not support him either. None of these four Republican leaders attended the RNC in July. Neither did former Trump rival, Ohio governor John Kasich. It was a clear snub, since the RNC was held in Kasich's home state.

Having become the presumptive nominee in May gave Trump a month's head start on general election campaigning over his Democratic rival. Former senator

After the RNC, Trump began campaigning for the general election. Along the campaign trail he spoke at packed rallies, such as this one in Loveland, Colorado, in October 2016.

and secretary of state Hillary Clinton had won the majority of the popular vote and delegate pledges in the Democratic primaries. However, her rival, Vermont senator Bernie Sanders, refused to concede until July 12.

During this extra time, experts expected Trump to consolidate support among all Republican and conservative voters. Instead, support for Trump waned. Primary voters hold more extreme opinions than American voters generally. The majority of registered voters across the country considered Trump unqualified to hold the nation's highest office.[1]

Trump was looking at his options for vice-president. He officially announced his running mate via Twitter on July 15, the Friday before the RNC. Trump chose Indiana governor Mike Pence as his running mate. Governor Pence was a social conservative with a long career in politics and a calm personality. He was a good complement to Trump's bombastic personality and lack of political experience.

Responding to Tragedy

Trump did not formally introduce Governor Pence until the following day. That's because a terrorist attack took the attention of the nation. On the evening of July 14,

Trump's family often joined him on the campaign trail, speaking on his behalf. *From left:* Tiffany, Donald Jr., Melania, Trump, Ivanka, and Eric with Donald's Jr.'s children, Kai and Donald III.

a terrorist killed more than 80 people in Nice, France. Police killed the attacker and charged his accomplices with terrorist conspiracy.

The attack on Nice was the latest in a rash of terrorist attacks in the United States and Europe. In June, a lone gunman had entered a nightclub in Orlando, Florida, and shot 49 people to death.[2] It was the deadliest terrorist attack in the United States since September 11, 2001. Before being shot by police, the gunman had pledged his support for ISIS, a Muslim militant group.

Terrorist attacks were not the only violent acts threatening American lives. On July 6, police officers in a Saint Paul, Minnesota, suburb shot and killed an unarmed African-American man, Philando Castile, during a traffic stop. The next day, a sniper opened fire on police officers in Dallas, Texas. He killed five officers before being killed himself by the Dallas police bomb squad.

In the wake of these attacks, Trump expanded on several of his campaign promises. In the aftermath of the Orlando shooting, Trump strengthened his position to ban Muslims from immigrating or visiting the United States. He also claimed to have foreseen the tragedy, stating, "I said this was going to happen—and it is only going to get worse."[3]

POLITICS AND TWITTER

Trump is an avid user of Twitter, a fast-paced social media platform. Twitter has transformed how Americans discuss politics and follow elections. It gives citizens access to candidates and other political figures and politicians direct access to the electorate. It also allows people with similar views to gather and air their grievances. For Trump, Twitter was an ideal way to immediately broadcast his policy positions, react to events, and criticize his opponents without having to answer questions from journalists. He announced his vice-presidential pick via Twitter, and often gave real-time reactions to events and his opponents over the platform.

After the Dallas shooting, Trump offered his sympathies to the families of the slain officers via Twitter. In a statement released soon after, he noted that the nation had become divided and racial tensions had gotten worse. He said that support for the police would help ensure every citizen felt safe and protected. After the attack in Nice, Trump reiterated the lack of respect he felt people had for law enforcement. "Here we go again," he said. "It's going to be a whole different world. . . . There is no respect for law and order."[4]

A Plan for the Future

Restoring law and order became a policy position for Trump at the RNC. The event prominently featured police officers and other law enforcement professionals and their families. He promised to restore law and order once he became president. He declared that attacks on law enforcement officers are attacks on the United States. Turning to terrorism overseas, Trump asserted that with him as president, the country would "defeat the barbarians of ISIS."[5]

On the last night of the RNC, Trump said, "To all Americans tonight, in all of our cities and in all of our towns, I make this promise: We will make America

Trump and Pence appeared to their delegates on the final night of the RNC.

strong again. We will make America proud again. We will make America safe again. And we will make America great again. God bless you and good night."[6] Now the official Republican nominee for president, Trump put the Republican primaries behind him and set his sights on the presumptive Democratic nominee, Hillary Clinton.

The morning after the RNC, Trump held a press conference. Despite media coverage on some of the failings of the RNC, including poor organization and gloomy themes, Trump praised the convention as "one of the best ever."[7] He thanked his staff and blasted Ted Cruz for failing to endorse him at the convention, saying it was dishonorable and asserting he did not want Cruz's endorsement. He ended by thanking his supporters and repeating his slogan, Make America Great Again.

Defining Positions on Trade and Treaties

As Trump began campaigning for the general election, he rolled out proposals for changing the trade deals and defense treaties the United States has with other countries. Trump promised to throw out the Trans-Pacific Partnership (TPP) deal President Obama negotiated with South Asian countries. He also

POLITICAL FACT-CHECKING

Prone to exaggerations and stretching the truth, Trump became a challenging candidate for the media to fact-check. Fact-checking is an important part of media coverage during a presidential election season. Several news organizations and independent groups fact-check the candidates. The *Tampa Bay Times* runs the website PolitiFact. PolitiFact uses what it calls a Truth-o-Meter to rate statements political figures make. Statements may be rated True, Mostly True, Half True, Mostly False, False, and Pants on Fire. The website provides an explanation for its rating and updates its ratings if politicians change their statements.

planned to renegotiate the North American Free Trade Agreement (NAFTA), a part of US trade policy since 1994. Doing so, he explained, would keep more jobs in the United States and put America first again.

Trump also planned to renegotiate defense treaties the United States has with other countries. The most notable of these was US participation in the North Atlantic Treaty Organization (NATO). The United States has been a member of NATO since the group began in 1949. Trump argued that the United States contributes much more in defense support than the other member nations, and that he would renegotiate the terms to get America a better deal. Until the other countries pay their fair share, Trump asserted, they may not get the help of the US military.

Fighting Clinton

After the RNC, Trump enjoyed a bump in the polls. He and the Republican Party had dominated news coverage during the RNC. But next came the Democratic Party's turn. Over the four days of the Democratic National Convention (DNC), party members, including President Barack Obama and Vice President Joe Biden, endorsed Hillary Clinton. She was voted the party nominee—and the first major party female presidential nominee in US history—on July 26.

Speakers at the DNC outlined their case against a Trump presidency. Some claimed Trump's outrageous personality made him unfit to be president. Clinton and others asserted that Trump's vision of America did not fit the ideals of the nation.

Like Trump, Clinton enjoyed a bump in the polls following the DNC. But the increased support did not last. Over August and September, Trump closed in on Clinton's lead. By the time of the first presidential debate on September 26, polls indicated the candidates were virtually tied. It was time for Trump and Clinton to come together on the same stage and persuade voters to support them.

"LOCK HER UP!"

Trump and the Republican Party spent much of the RNC making the case why Clinton was unfit to be president. On the second night, New Jersey governor Chris Christie took the stage as the crowds chanted, "Lock Her Up!"[8] He disparaged Clinton's work as secretary of state. Her handling of classified information on a private e-mail server set up in her home became the focus of intense criticism, as did her leadership in the wake of an attack on US diplomats in Benghazi, Libya. These criticisms would remain talking points through the rest of the election.

CHAPTER
NINE

RACE TO ELECTION DAY

Trump and Clinton took the debate stage at New York's Hofstra University on September 26. Lester Holt moderated the discussion between the two candidates. The polls had narrowed between Trump and Clinton, who were now just two points apart, with Clinton enjoying a narrow lead. It was time for Trump to convince the American people to vote for him.

Trump and Clinton Take the Stage

The debate at Hofstra University was divided into six segments on the issues facing the United States. Among the topics were the economy, national security, and foreign policy. Trump and Clinton did not receive the questions ahead of time. But historically, presidential candidates spend weeks preparing for the debate, reading up on the issues and preparing arguments against opponents' talking points. This is the approach

Trump answers questions in a town hall meeting in Sandown, New Hampshire, in October 2016.

Trump and Clinton expressed their views at the first presidential debate in September 2016.

Clinton took leading up to September 26, but Trump was an unconventional candidate. He was confident that his experience speaking on television and at rallies would be enough preparation.

Through the 95-minute debate, Trump painted Clinton as a longtime politician who was out of touch with regular Americans. He upbraided her for her use of a private e-mail server during her term as secretary of state. Trump criticized Clinton's stance on free trade, saying he would eliminate trade deals with other nations. But then, Clinton began to strike back. She confronted Trump on his support of the Iraq War and his longstanding claims that President Obama was born outside the United States, despite evidence to the contrary. Trump's lack of preparation began to show. After the night was over, most political experts agreed that Clinton had won the debate. However, debate wins typically matter little to voters.

Despite his performance on September 26, Trump did not change his approach to the second and third debates. The second debate was a town hall format, with undecided voters sitting onstage with the candidates. The voters asked the candidates questions on a range of issues. While answering these questions, Trump landed

WHAT IS A TOWN HALL DEBATE?

The second 2016 presidential debate had a town hall format. In addition to the moderators asking candidates questions, audience members posed questions to the candidates. The audience was a group of undecided voters. They asked questions on a range of topics, from health care to the rise of Islamophobia in the United States.

The town hall style has been a presidential debate format since 1992. It allows voters to have a direct say in the issues candidates discuss. Candidates do not get to see the questions ahead of time. For this reason, voters and debate viewers consider candidates' answers to town hall debate questions more authentic than their prepared opening and closing remarks during other debates. Instead of standing behind podiums, candidates can walk around a circular stage surrounded by the audience. This makes audience interaction part of the debate. Sometimes, how a candidate interacts with the debate audience determines which candidate wins the debate.

strikes against Clinton once again on her use of a private e-mail server as secretary of state. But Clinton had continued to prepare for the second and third debates. She was once again declared the winner of both.

October Surprises

In presidential elections, campaigns often wait until the last few weeks to release unsavory information about their opponents. This information is informally called an October surprise. For Trump, October was full of surprises. During the first debate, Clinton landed a barb that stuck. She criticized Trump for calling a former Miss Universe pageant winner "Miss Piggy" after she gained weight following the competition.[1] The comment rattled Trump, who was not expecting the attack. The next morning, Trump called into a morning talk show to defend his statements about the Miss Universe winner.

While the Miss Universe story was still fresh, the *New York Times* published a story on Trump's taxes. Trump had refused to release his tax returns because he was under a tax audit. An anonymous source supplied the newspaper with evidence that Trump claimed a $916 million loss in 1995.[2] Some reporters claimed that under the tax laws, Trump may not have paid income tax for nearly 20 years despite being wealthy.[3] Then, a few days later, an 11-year-old tape of an *Access Hollywood* TV show segment surfaced. The tape caught Trump having a lewd conversation about women with the show's host.

The content of the tape was shocking and offensive to many voters and Republican officials. Trump apologized for his comments. He also asserted to Hillary Clinton that her husband, former president Bill Clinton, had treated women much worse. Over the next few days, nearly 20 percent of Republican governors and Republican members of the US Congress withdrew their support of Trump.[4] Some went so far as to call for Trump to step down as the presidential nominee. But Trump refused to do so. He told reporters at the *Washington Post,* "I'd never withdraw. I've never

EARLY VOTING

Election Day is always the Tuesday after the first Monday of November, but many Americans cast their votes well before then. Most states offer early voting to some or all of their registered voters. Voters do not need a reason to vote early, and they can even vote early if they would be able to get to the polls on Election Day. States determine how early voting begins. Some states allow voting up to 45 days before Election Day. Others do not offer early voting at all.

withdrawn in my life. No, I'm not quitting this race. I have tremendous support."[5]

While several surprises rattled the Trump campaign, Clinton also faced a few surprises of her own. Before the second debate, Trump held a press conference with four women. Three of the women had accused Bill of treating them inappropriately. The fourth was a child when Clinton worked as a defense lawyer for a man who had attacked her. Then, a week before the general election, FBI director James Comey revealed the bureau had found additional Clinton e-mails on one of her aide's computers. The revelation caused Clinton, who had led in the polls after the third debate, to stumble. By the eve of the election, Clinton's lead had narrowed. It was time for American voters to pick their next president.

Election Day

On November 7, the day before Election Day, most polls favored Clinton. But the Trump campaign remained cautiously optimistic about its chances. Throughout the election season, Trump had defied expectations. From the morning he announced his candidacy, political experts had predicted Trump would not be successful. But he had beat 16 competitors in the Republican primary season, mobilizing a base of voters who felt politicians did not represent them, disagreed with the path the country was on, and demanded change. Would these voters come out in enough numbers to give Trump the win?

On November 8, Americans took to their voting booths to cast their votes for president. At 6:00 p.m. eastern standard time, the first results of the election began to come in. Trump took an early lead in states that were expected to go to the Republican nominee. But then the vote tallies in key battleground states—those either candidate might win that would likely decide the presidency—started coming in. Florida, Virginia, and North Carolina were expected to go narrowly to Clinton. But early results showed Trump taking the lead in those states.

ELECTION POLLING

Trump's upset victory over Clinton turned a lot of what was considered conventional wisdom on political polling on its head. Polling experts across the nation and across political ideologies all predicted Clinton would win on November 8. But Trump outperformed his expectations. After the elections, pollsters analyzed their methods to understand how they could have missed Trump's victory. Early analysis pointed to flaws in how pollsters collected their data, including the number of men and women included in a poll and proportion of white voters to voters of color polled. If these numbers do not realistically reflect the voting public, polls will not be accurate.

As election results continued to pour in, it became clear that polls and political experts had been wrong about Clinton's lead, and the election would be much closer than expected. Then, Trump began to rack up votes in states that had been considered safe bets for Clinton, including Pennsylvania, Michigan, and Wisconsin. The cautious optimism of the Trump campaign turned into enthusiastic hope.

Election night continued into the early hours of November 9. As state after state returned its election results, it became clear Trump was winning in an upset. Just after 2:00 a.m. eastern standard time, Trump led Clinton in electoral votes, which would decide the outcome of the election. He was only five electoral votes away from winning the election. Then, the final vote tally came in for the state of Wisconsin. The state went for Trump, giving him the 270 electoral votes he needed to win. Although Clinton ultimately won the popular vote nationally by a thin margin, Trump was the president-elect of the United States.

Shortly after Trump reached 270, Clinton called him to concede the election. Then, Trump took the stage at his New York City campaign headquarters to greet his supporters and give his victory speech.

Trump gave his acceptance speech early on Wednesday, November 9, with Barron and Melania at his side.

He began his speech praising Clinton on a hard-fought campaign and thanked his family, his campaign staff, and his supporters. But the substance of his speech was addressed to the American people. His movement was just beginning, he said, including the "urgent task of rebuilding our nation and renewing the American dream."[6]

TIMELINE

1946
Donald John Trump is born on June 14 in
Jamaica Estates, Queens, New York.

1968
Trump graduates from the Wharton School of Business
at the University of Pennsylvania on May 20.

1973
Trump Management Corporation is sued on October
15 for violating the Fair Housing Act of 1968.

1977
On April 9, Trump marries Ivana Winklmayr; their son,
Donald John Trump Jr., is born on December 31.

1980
The Grand Hyatt opens in New York City.

1981
Ivanka Trump is born on October 30.

1982
Seven hundred guests toast the near completion of Trump Tower in July; Trump begins construction on Trump Plaza in Atlantic City, New Jersey.

1984
Eric Trump is born on January 6.

1987
Trump hosts the release party for his book *The Art of the Deal* on December 12.

TIMELINE

1990
Ivana and Donald announce they are divorcing in January.

1993
Tiffany Trump is born on October 13; Trump marries Marla Maples in December.

1999
Donald and Marla formally divorce on June 8; Fred Trump dies at age 93 on June 25.

2004
The first episode of *The Apprentice* airs on January 8.

2005
Trump marries Melania Knauss on January 22; Trump University opens.

2006
Barron Trump is born on March 20.

2013
The New York attorney general sues Trump and his companies over alleged fraud involving Trump University.

2015
Trump announces his candidacy for president of the United States on June 16.

2016
Trump becomes the Republican front-runner after winning 7 of 11 primary contests on Super Tuesday on March 1; Trump becomes the presumptive Republican nominee for president after his last opponent, Governor John Kasich, drops out on May 4; The Republican National Convention is held in Cleveland, Ohio, from July 18–21; Trump becomes the official Republican nominee for president on July 21; Trump is elected the forty-fifth president on November 8.

ESSENTIAL FACTS

Date of Birth
June 14, 1946

Place of Birth
Jamaica Estates, Queens, New York

Parents
Fred Trump and Mary Anne Trump

Education
New York Military Academy; Fordham University;
University of Pennsylvania's Wharton School of Business

Marriages
Ivana Winklmayr (1977–1990), Marla Maples (1993–1999),
Melania Knauss (2005–)

Children
Donald Jr., Ivanka, Eric, Tiffany, Barron

Career Highlights
Trump's career began with real estate development in New York City, New York, including the Commodore Hotel and Trump Tower. In the early 1980s, Trump opened three large luxury casinos in Atlantic City, New Jersey. Trump's reality television show, *The Apprentice*, premiered in 2004. In 2016, he was elected 45th president of the United States.

Societal Contributions

Trump renovated rundown buildings in New York City, revitalizing the surrounding neighborhoods and providing jobs for thousands during the projects.

Conflicts

In 1973, Trump's company faced a lawsuit for violating the Fair Housing Act. The lawsuit was settled, stating the company did not commit any wrongdoing. During construction for Trump Tower, Trump's company destroyed historic carvings, angering art lovers. Trump's company also faced a lawsuit for employing illegal immigrants.

On the campaign trail, Trump's proposals to ban Muslim immigration and build a wall on the US-Mexico border met with conflict. Tapes of Trump making lewd comments about women drew the anger of Republicans and Democrats alike.

Quote

"When I take the oath of office next year, I will restore law and order to our country. . . . In this race to the White House, I am the Law and Order candidate."—*Donald Trump, 2016 Republican National Convention*

GLOSSARY

abatement
A deduction.

antiestablishment
Against the existing political structure and culture.

asset
An item of value.

conservative
Believing in small government and established social, economic, and political traditions and practices.

convention
A gathering of members of a political party that meets to select a candidate to run for office.

delegate
A person sent to a convention to represent a group or a state.

draft
A system in which people of a certain age are required to register for military service.

ghostwrite
To write for someone else who is the assumed author.

interest
A fee charged when a person or business borrows money.

liberal
Believing in large government and supporting new ideas and ways of behaving.

moderate
A person who holds political or religious beliefs that are not extreme.

plagiarized
To have copied and claimed another person's words or ideas as your own.

presumptive
Probable.

primary
A political contest political parties hold to determine their presidential nominees.

rhetoric
Language intended to influence people, even if it may not be completely truthful.

Social Security
A US program started in the 1930s to provide retirement income for people over the age of 65.

ADDITIONAL RESOURCES

Selected Bibliography

Andrews, Wilson, Kitty Bennett, and Alicia Parlapiano. "2016 Delegate Count and Primary Results." *Election 2016*. New York Times, 5 July 2016. Web. 8 Nov. 2016.

Blair, Gwenda. *The Trumps: Three Generations That Built an Empire*. New York: Simon, 2000. Print.

"Donald J. Trump Republican Nomination Acceptance Speech." *DonaldJTrump.com*. Donald J. Trump for President, Inc. 21 July 2016. Web. 8 Nov. 2016.

"Political Polarization in the American Public." *US Politics & Policy*. Pew Research Center, 12 June 2014. Web. 8 Nov. 2016.

Further Readings

Dillon, Patrick. *The Story of Buildings*. Somerville, MA: Candlewick, 2014. Print.

Sobel, Syl. *Presidential Elections and Other Cool Facts*. Hauppauge, NY: Barron's, 2016. Print.

Websites

To learn more about Essential Lives, visit **booklinks.abdopublishing.com**. These links are routinely monitored and updated to provide the most current information available.

Places to Visit

National Republican Committee
310 1st Street SE
Washington, DC 20003
202-863-8500
http://www.gop.com
The official website of the Republican Party has information
on the party and Donald Trump's campaign.

Trump Tower New York
725 5th Avenue
New York, New York 10022
212-836-3226
http://trumptowerny.com
Learn about the history of Trump Tower in New York City.

The White House
1600 Pennsylvania Avenue NW
Washington, DC 20500
202-456-1111
http://www.whitehouse.gov
Visit the official website of the White House or the
White House itself to learn more about the history of the
presidency.

SOURCE NOTES

Chapter 1. Convention in Cleveland

1. CBS News. "Donald Trump's Dramatic RNC Entrance." *YouTube*. YouTube, 18 July 2016. Web. 31 Oct. 2016.

2. "Beyond Distrust: How Americans View Their Government." *Pew Research Center*. Pew Research Center, 23 Nov. 2015. Web. 22 July 2016.

3. Lee Horwich, Beryl Love, John Brecher, Amalie Nash, ed. "Trump Nation." *USA Today*. USA Today, n.d. Web. 31 Oct. 2016.

4. Reuters with amNY.com staff. "Melania Trump's RNC Speech: Meredith McIver, Trump Organization Staff Writer, Takes Responsibility." *amNewYork*. Newsday, 20 July 2016. Web. 31 Oct. 2016.

5. Theodore Schleifer and Stephen Collinson. "Defiant Ted Cruz Stands by Refusal to Endorse Trump after Being Booed during Convention Speech." *CNN.com*. Cable News Network, 22 July 2016. Web. 5 Oct. 2016.

6. Greg Krieg, Will Mullery, and Tal Yellin. "How to Become a Republican Delegate." Politics. *CNN.com*. Cable News Network, 27 Apr. 2016. Web. 31 Oct. 2016.

7. "Donald J. Trump Republican Nomination Acceptance Speech." *DonaldJTrump.com*. Donald J. Trump for President, 21 July 2016. Web. 31 Oct. 2016.

8. Ibid.

9. Ibid.

Chapter 2. Growing Up Trump

1. Gwenda Blair. *The Trumps: Three Generations That Built an Empire*. New York: Simon, 2000. Print. 225.

2. Ibid. 235.

3. Donald J. Trump. *The Art of the Deal*. New York: Random, 1987. Print. 78.

4. Ibid. 78.

5. Steve Eder and Dave Phillips. "Donald Trump's Draft Deferments: Four for College, One for Bad Feet." *New York Times*. New York Times, 1 Aug. 2016. Web. 31 Oct. 2016.

6. Gwenda Blair. *The Trumps: Three Generations That Built an Empire*. New York: Simon, 2000. Print. 246.

Chapter 3. Building New York

1. David W. Dunlap. "1973: Meet Donald Trump." *New York Times*. New York Times, 30 July 2015. Web. 29 Sept. 2016.

2. Tracie Rozhon. "Fred C. Trump, Postwar Master Builder of Housing for Middle Class, Dies at 93." *New York Times*. New York Times, 26 June 1999. Web. 16 June 2016.

3. David W. Dunlap. "1973: Meet Donald Trump." *New York Times*. New York Times, 30 July 2015. Web. 29 Sept. 2016.

4. "The Grand Hyatt Hotel." *The Trump Organization*. The Trump Organization, 2016. Web. 31 Oct. 2016.

5. "Donald J. Trump Biography." *The Trump Organization*. The Trump Organization, 2016. Web. 31 Oct. 2016.

6. Callum Borchers. "Donald Trump Hasn't Changed One Bit Since His First Media Feud in 1980." *Washington Post*. Washington Post, 18 Mar. 2016. Web. 31 Oct. 2016.

7. David Freedlander. "A 1980s New York City Battle Explains Donald Trump's Candidacy." *Bloomberg Politics*. Bloomberg LP, 29 Sept. 2015. Web. 20 July 2016.

8. Gwenda Blair. *The Trumps: Three Generations That Built an Empire*. New York: Simon, 2000. Print. 314–315.

9. Ibid. 325.

Chapter 4. Gambling on the Future

1. Gwenda Blair. *The Trumps: Three Generations That Built an Empire*. New York: Simon, 2000. Print. 101.

2. Charles V. Bagli. "Trump Group Selling West Side Parcel for $1.8 Billion." *New York Times*. New York Times, 1 June 2005. Web. 31 Oct. 2016.

3. Gwenda Blair. *The Trumps: Three Generations That Built an Empire*. New York: Simon, 2000. Print. 365.

4. Mark Singer. "Trump Solo." *New Yorker*. Condé Nast, 19 May 1997. Web. 16 June 2016.

5. David Segal. "What Donald Trump's Plaza Deal Reveals about His White House Bid." *New York Times*. New York Times, 16 Jan. 2016. Web. 8 Oct. 2016.

6. Gwenda Blair. *The Trumps: Three Generations That Built an Empire*. New York: Simon, 2000. Print. 390–391.

7. Ibid.

8. Monica Langley. "Donald Trump's Complex Business Ties Could Set a New Precedent; Conflict-of-Interest Question Would Loom Large if the Republican Is Elected." *Wall Street Journal*. Dow Jones, 4 July 2016. Web. 31 Oct. 2016.

9. Jane Mayer. "Donald Trump's Ghostwriter Tells All." *New Yorker*. Condé Nast, 25 July 2016. Web. 14 Oct. 2016.

10. Gwenda Blair. *The Trumps: Three Generations That Built an Empire*. New York: Simon, 2000. Print. 381.

Chapter 5. Building the Brand

1. Gwenda Blair. *The Trumps: Three Generations That Built an Empire*. New York: Simon 2000. Print. 382–389.

2. David A Graham. "The Many Scandals of Donald Trump: A Cheat Sheet." *The Atlantic.com*. Atlantic Monthly Group, 9 June 2016. Web. 31 Oct. 2016.

3. Ibid.

4. Ibid.

5. Ibid.

6. "40 Wall Street: The Trump Building." *40WallStreet.com*. 40 Wall Street, n.d. Web. 31 Oct. 2016.

7. Charles V. Bagli. "Trump Sells Hyatt Share to Pritzkers." *New York Times*. New York Times, 8 Oct. 1996. Web. 20 July 2016.

8. Donald J. Trump. *Trump: The Art of the Comeback*. New York: Times, 1997. *New York Times Books*. Web. 9 Nov. 2016.

9. Charles V. Bagli. "Trump Sells Hyatt Share to Pritzkers." *New York Times*. New York Times, 8 Oct. 1996. Web. 20 July 2016.

SOURCE NOTES CONTINUED

10. Tracie Rozhon. "Fred C. Trump, Postwar Master Builder of Housing for Middle Class, Dies at 93." *New York Times*. New York Times, 26 June 1999. Web. 8 Nov. 2016.

Chapter 6. Branching Out

1. "The Political Fray: The 1992 Run for the Presidency." *All Politics: CNN & Time*. AllPolitics, 1996. Web. 31 Oct. 2016.

2. Marc Fisher. "Donald Trump, Remade by Reality TV." *Washington Post*, Washington Post, 27 Jan. 2016. Web. 16 June 2016.

3. Amy Bingham. "Donald Trump's Companies Filed for Bankruptcy 4 Times." *ABC News*. ABC News, 21 Apr. 2011. Web. 1 Nov. 2016.

4. Ibid.

5. Ibid.

6. "Trump International Hotel and Tower." *Chicago Architecture Info*. Artefacts Corporation, 2016. Web. 31 Oct. 2016.

7. John Cassidy. "Trump University: It's Worse Than You Think." *New Yorker*. Condé Nast, 2 June 2016. 1 Nov. 2016.

8. Ibid.

9. Scott Clement and Philip Rucker. "In New Poll, Support for Trump Has Plunged, Giving Clinton a Double-Digit Lead." *Washington Post*. Washington Post, 26 June 2016. Web. 31 Oct. 2016.

10. Shannon Travis. "Was He Ever Serious? How Trump Strung the Country Along, Again." *CNN.com*. Cable News Network, 17 May 2011. Web. 31 Oct. 2016.

11. Ibid.

Chapter 7. Make America Great Again

1. "Here's Donald Trump's Presidential Announcement Speech." *Time*. Time, 16 June 2016. Web. 1 Nov. 2016.

2. Nate Cohn. "The One Demographic That Is Hurting Hillary Clinton." *New York Times*. New York Times, 25 July 2016. Web. 1 Nov. 2016.

3. "San Bernardino Shooting Victims: Who They Were." *Los Angeles Times*. Los Angeles Times, 17 Dec. 2015. Web. 1 Nov. 2016.

4. Jeremy Diamond. "Donald Trump: Ban All Muslim Travel to US." *CNN.com*. Cable News Network, 8 Dec. 2015. Web. 14 Oct. 2016.

5. Alicia Parlapiano. "Stacking Up the Presidential Fields." *New York Times*. New York Times, 12 Feb. 2016. Web. 20 July 2016.

6. Ibid.

7. Donald J. Trump. *The Art of the Deal*. New York: Random, 1987. Print. 56.

8. "Iowa Caucus Results." *New York Times*. New York Times, 17 June 2016. Web. 20 July 2016.

9. Wilson Andrews, Kitty Bennett, and Alicia Parlapiano. "2016 Delegate Count and Primary Results." *New York Times*. New York Times, 5 July 2016. Web. 20 July 2016.

10. Ibid.

11. Ibid.

12. Ibid.

13. Dylan Byers. "Donald Trump Has Earned $2 Billion in Free Media Coverage, Study Shows." *CNN.com*. Cable News Network, 15 Mar. 2016. Web. 26 July 2016.

14. Jack Shafer. "Donald Trump's Phony War on the Press." *Politico Magazine*. Politico, 6 June 2016. Web. 1 Nov. 2016.

15. Philip Rucker. "Trump Says Fox's Megyn Kelly Had 'Blood Coming Out of Her Wherever.'" *Washington Post*. Washington Post, 8 Aug. 2015. Web. 20 July 2016.

16. Nick Gass. "The 21 Craziest Quotes from the Campaign Trail." *Politico Magazine*. Politico, 25 Nov. 2015. Web. 20 July 2016.

Chapter 8. The Campaign Trail

1. Emily Guskin and Scott Clement. "Most Voters Say Donald Trump Isn't Qualified—But Some of Them Are Backing Him Anyway. Here's Why." *Washington Post*. Washington Post, 19 July 2016. Web. 1 Nov. 2016.

2. Ashley Ellis, Faith Karimi, and Eliott C. McLaughlin. "Orlando Shooting: 49 Killed, Shooter Pledged ISIS Allegiance." *CNN.com*. Cable News Network, 13 June 2016. Web. 26 July 2016.

3. Jonathan Martin. "Donald Trump Seizes on Orlando Shooting and Repeats Call for Temporary Ban on Muslim Migration." *New York Times*. New York Times, 12 June 2016. Web. 26 July 2016.

4. Reena Flores. "Clinton, Trump React to France Attack." *CBS News*. CBS Interactive, 14 July 2016. Web. 1 Nov. 2016.

5. "Donald J. Trump Republican Nomination Acceptance Speech." *DonaldJTrump.com*. Donald J. Trump for President, Inc., 21 July 2016. Web. 31 Oct. 2016.

6. Ibid.

7. Chris Cillizza. "Donald Trump Just Gave Another Absolutely Epic Press Conference." *Washington Post*. Washington Post, 22 July 2016. Web. 25 July 2016.

8. Michael D. Shear and David E. Sanger. "Chris Christie Made a Case against Hillary Clinton. We Fact-Checked." *New York Times*. New York Times, 20 July 2016. Web. 25 July 2016.

Chapter 9. Race to Election Day

1. Matea Gold, Anne Gearan, and Philip Rucker. "Trump Says He May Hit 'Harder' in Next Debate; Clinton Tells Reporters She Had a 'Great, Great Time.'" *Washington Post*. Washington Post, 27 Sept. 2016. Web. 18 Oct. 2016.

2. David Barstow, Susanne Craig, Russ Buettner, and Megan Twohey. "Donald Trump Tax Records Show He Could Have Avoided Taxes for Nearly Two Decades, The Times Found." *New York Times*. New York Times, 1 Oct. 2016. Web. 18 Oct. 2016.

3. Ibid.

4. David Johnson and Chris Wilson. "Which Republicans Have Stopped Supporting Donald Trump?" *Time*. Time, Oct. 12, 2016. Web. 18 Oct. 2016.

5. Robert Costa. "Amid Growing Calls to Drop Out, Trump Vows to 'Never Withdraw.'" *Washington Post*. Washington Post, 8 Oct. 2016. Web. 8 Nov. 2016.

6. Federal News Services. "Transcript: Donald Trump's Victory Speech." *New York Times*. New York Times, 9 Nov. 2016. Web. 9 Nov. 2016.

INDEX

ABOUT THE AUTHOR

A. R. Carser is a freelance writer who lives in Minnesota. She follows local, state, and national politics closely and found the 2016 presidential election fascinating.